THEMATIC UNIT
Months and Seasons

Written By Diann Culver

Teacher Created Materials, Inc.
6421 Industry Way
Westminster, CA 92683
www.teachercreated.com

ISBN-0-7439-3106-8

©2004 Teacher Created Materials, Inc.

Made in U.S.A.

Illustrated by
Alexandra Artigas

Edited by
Kim Fields

Cover Art by
Anthony Carrillo

Teacher Created Materials

Table of Contents

Introduction

Months and Seasons is a captivating, comprehensive thematic unit. Its 80 exciting pages are filled with a wide variety of lesson ideas designed for use with primary school children. At its core are two high-quality children's literature selections, *Chicken Soup with Rice* and *The Apple Pie Tree*. For these books, activities are included which set the stage for reading, encourage the enjoyment of the books, and extend the concepts gained. In addition, the theme is connected to the curriculum with activities in language arts (including daily writing suggestions), math, science, social studies, art, music, and movement. Many of these activities encourage cooperative learning. Suggestions and patterns for bulletin boards and unit-management tools are additional time savers for the busy teacher. Furthermore, culminating activities are included, which allow children to synthesize their knowledge.

This thematic unit includes:

- ❏ **literature selections**—summaries of two children's books with related lessons (complete with reproducible pages) that cross the curriculum

- ❏ **poetry**—suggested selections and a poem outline enabling children to write and publish their own works

- ❏ **planning guides**—suggestions for sequencing lessons each day of the unit

- ❏ **writing ideas**—daily suggestions as well as writing activities across the curriculum

- ❏ **bulletin board ideas**—suggestions and plans for child-created and/or interactive bulletin boards

- ❏ **curriculum connections**—in language arts, math, science, social studies, art, music, and movement

- ❏ **group projects**—to foster cooperative learning

- ❏ **culminating activities**—which require children to synthesize their learning to produce a product or engage in an activity that can be shared with others

- ❏ **a bibliography**—suggesting additional fiction and nonfiction books on the theme

> To keep this valuable resource intact so that it can be used year after year, you may wish to punch holes in the pages and store them in a three-ring binder.

Introduction *(cont.)*

Why a Balanced Approach?

The strength of a balanced language approach is that it involves children in using all modes of communication—reading, writing, listening, illustrating, and doing. Communication skills are interconnected and integrated into lessons that emphasize the whole of language. Implicit in this approach is our knowledge that every whole—including individual words—is composed of parts, and directed study of those parts can help a child to master the whole. Experience and research tell us that regular attention to phonics, other word-attack skills, and spelling develops reading mastery, thereby fulfilling the unity of the whole language experience. The child is thus led to read, write, spell, speak, and listen more confidently.

Why Thematic Planning?

One very useful tool for implementing an integrated language program is thematic planning. By choosing a theme with a correlating literature selection for a unit of study, a teacher can plan activities throughout the day that lead to a cohesive, in-depth study of the topic. Children will be practicing and applying their skills in meaningful context. Consequently, they tend to learn and retain more.

Why Cooperative Learning?

Besides academic skills and content, children need to learn social skills. No longer can this area of development be taken for granted. Children must learn to work cooperatively in groups in order to function well in modern society. Group activities should be a regular part of school life, and teachers should consciously include social objectives as well as academic objectives in their planning.

Chicken Soup with Rice

by Maurice Sendak

Summary

Chicken Soup with Rice *is a book about the months of the year. Each of the twelve months is described in rhyming verse. This book is easy to follow, and children will enjoy the different ways the narrator encounters chicken soup with rice as he travels through the year.*

The outline below is a suggested plan for using the various activities presented in this unit. You should adapt these ideas to fit your classroom situation.

Sample Plan

Day 1

- Introduce the unit using the Birthday Bulletin Board (pages 10–11).
- Complete the Vocabulary Development for *Chicken Soup with Rice* (page 7, #2).
- Read *Chicken Soup with Rice*.
- Complete the Rhyming Words Chart and related activity (page 7, #4).
- Complete the Rhyme Chimes and Rhyming Words (pages 12–14).

Day 2

- Read *Chicken Soup with Rice*.
- Begin the Learning Calendar and continue to use each day (page 22).
- Do Monthly Match (page 17).
- Complete the Ordinal Number Pocket Chart (pages 15–16).
- Teach the traditional poem, "Thirty Days Hath September" (page 8, #9).
- Complete How Many Days? (pages 18–19).

Day 3

- Read *Chicken Soup with Rice*.
- Review the months of the year.
- Choral read, "Birthday Poem" (page 20).
- Complete the large Birthday Graph and compare the number of birthdays in each month (page 8, #11).
- Complete the Independent Birthday Graph (page 21).

Day 4

- Read *Chicken Soup with Rice*.
- Complete the Learning Calendar and School-Year Calendar writing activity (page 22–24).
- Complete an Author Study on Maurice Sendak; read other books by him (page 9, #1).
- Create invitations and placemats (page 9, #4 and #5).

Day 5

- Read *Chicken Soup with Rice*.
- Make chicken soup (page 25).
- Write the recipe for chicken soup (page 26).

Overview of Activities

SETTING THE STAGE

1. The Birthday Bulletin Board will help students learn the months of the year and keep up with class birthdays. The bulletin board should be displayed throughout the school year.

Use pages 10–11 to create picture symbols for the Birthday Bulletin Board. Enlarge the symbols, then color, cut out, and laminate them. The picture symbols must be large enough for students to see and understand. The symbols will help students associate each month with a holiday or another event that happens during that month. Mount the symbols on a bulletin board or wall.

Ask each student to bring a small photograph of himself or herself to school. Teachers may want to ask parents for a picture before school begins and have the display ready before school starts. This will make students feel welcome and comfortable during their first days at school.

Make several copies of the birthday cake on page 10 and mount each student's picture on a cake. Then fill in the information. Add the birthday cakes to the Birthday Bulletin Board according to the students' birthdays. Begin the year by introducing the picture symbols on the Birthday Bulletin Board and associating the symbols with the months and the students' birthdays. At the beginning of each month, review the bulletin board and call attention to the students who have birthdays during that month.

2. Make a Rhyming Words Chart from bulletin-board paper to use with *Chicken Soup with Rice*. (See Appendix: Rhyming Words Chart.)

3. Copy a Rhyme Chimes pattern (page 12) for each student. Write a different word ending and example at the top of each bell. Prepare enough bells so that each child has one. Use the list on page 13 for endings and corresponding word examples that can be used. Be sure to use word endings that are suitable for the age group you teach.

4. To prepare an Ordinal Number Chart, color, cut out, and laminate the pictures that correspond with each month on pages 15–16. Cut 12 sentence strips into three parts. Write the ordinal number (1st–12th) on the first part of the strip, the name of the month on the second part, and the season of the year on the third part. Laminate the strips for durability. (See Appendix: Ordinal Number Chart.) Complete a pocket chart in advance to use with this activity.

5. Write the "Birthday Poem" (page 20) on chart paper and laminate it.

6. Prepare the Birthday Graph (see format on page 21) by cutting bulletin-board paper into twelve 2" x 24" (5 cm x 61 cm) strips.

Overview of Activities *(cont.)*

ENJOYING THE BOOK

1. Introduce the book *Chicken Soup with Rice* to the students. Read the title and the author's name. Tell the students that Maurice Sendak has written and illustrated many books. The students might recognize the following two titles: *Where the Wild Things Are* and *In the Night Kitchen*.

2. Explain that the book *Chicken Soup with Rice* introduces some special words that the students may not have heard before. Tell them that authors use special words to make their stories and poems more interesting and to help the reader imagine a picture in his or her mind about the story. Introduce the special words used in the story. (See Appendix: Vocabulary Development—Special Words.) Brainstorm synonyms for the words before reading the story. Read the book through once for enjoyment.

3. After reading the book once, explain that this book is written in poetry form. Tell the students to listen closely for rhyming words as you read the book a second time. Read the book one page at a time and have students raise their hands to tell you the rhyming words they hear on that page. List the rhyming words beside each month on the Rhyming Words Chart.

4. After all the rhyming words are listed on the chart, have the students identify how the words are alike and different. Underline the endings of each set of rhyming words to show students that rhyming words must sound alike at the end, but the words may or may not be spelled alike. (See Appendix: Rhyming Words Chart.)

5. Introduce the Rhyme Chimes activity (page 12) by writing the following ending word patterns on the board or a chart: *at, ed, in, og, un*. Have the students add a consonant letter or letters to the beginning of each word pattern to create a word. Divide the students into groups of two or three. Give each child a Rhyme Chimes bell shape (prepared in advance). Then give the child a different colored marker and say that he or she is the only one who can write on that bell, but the group members may help one another with ideas for words. The teacher can set a specific number of words that the student must write on the bell. Tell the students to work together to complete all the bells and emphasize that all of the bells in a group must be completed before the activity is finished. When the groups are finished, allow each child to read the words on his or her bell to check for accuracy. Display the Rhyme Chime bells in the hall or around the classroom.

6. Extend the Rhyme Chime activity using Rhyming Words as an independent activity (page 14).

7. To create the Ordinal Number Chart, identify each month and its corresponding ordinal number as you read *Chicken Soup with Rice* again. Discuss each month by identifying holidays, weather, the season, students who have birthdays in that month, etc. (Refer to the Birthday Bulletin Board

Overview of Activities *(cont.)*

ENJOYING THE BOOK *(cont.)*

on pages 10–11 for students' birthdays.) Introduce the month pictures (pages 15–16) that you laminated earlier and have students match each picture to a month of the year. Practice saying the months in order; emphasize that months of the year are identified with ordinal numbers such as first, second, and third. Put the first ordinal number strip into the pocket chart and ask the children to identify the first month of the year and add the January strip to the pocket chart. Continue the activity until each of the twelve months has been added to the pocket chart with its corresponding ordinal number beside the month. Call the students' attention to the weather that occurs in each month and place the season name in the chart beside the month and ordinal number. Emphasize the four seasons and the months that go with each season. Match the pictures used earlier in the activity to each month and add those to the pocket chart. (See Appendix: Ordinal Number Chart.) Repeat this activity several times until students recognize the twelve months, the ordinal numbers, and the seasons. This activity may also be used in a learning center.

(**Note:** There are several skills included in this activity. Teachers may wish to break the activity into smaller parts to use with younger students.)

8. Practice reciting the months of the year and ordinal numbers (first to twelfth) every day. Students should be able to recite them all before attempting this next activity. In random order, write all of the months and the ordinal numbers on the board or a chart. Use Monthly Match on page 17 to evaluate student learning.

9. Have students recite the traditional poem, "Thirty Days Hath September," shown below. Discuss the meaning of the poem—emphasizing the number of days in each month. Tell the students that many people use the poem to help them remember how many days are in each month. Post the poem in the classroom. Extend the activity using How Many Days? on pages 18–19. Model the activity on the board and then assign the pages as an independent activity.

Thirty days hath September, April, June, and November;

February has twenty-eight alone, All the rest have thirty-one,

Excepting leap year, that's the time, When February's days are twenty-nine.

10. Read the "Birthday Poem" (page 20) to students (prepared in advance). Choral read it with the students and then discuss the students' birthday months. Assign the students to small groups according to their birthdays. Have each group read the line in the poem that refers to its birthday month. All of the students read the last line of each verse, and they all read the last verse together. They will end the poem by saying their birthdays. The teacher can read those months that do not have any birthdays. Do this activity several times before going on to the Birthday Graph.

11. Group the students according to their birthdays to make the large Birthday Graph. Give each group one of the 2" x 24" (5 cm x 61 cm) bulletin-board paper strips cut earlier. Give each group rulers, markers, and crayons. Have the groups divide the paper into 2" (5 cm) squares using a pencil and tracing over the lines with a marker, making it 12 squares long. Have each child color one square to represent his or her birthday. Glue each strip, in order, onto the Birthday Bulletin Board next to the month it represents. The teacher should glue a plain strip on each month that has no birthdays.

Overview of Activities *(cont.)*

ENJOYING THE BOOK *(cont.)*

12. Compare the number of birthdays in each month using the following questions: How many birthdays are in (name each month)? Which month has the most birthdays? Which month has the least birthdays? Do any months have the same number of birthdays? Create addition and subtraction sentences using the chart for a whole group activity.

13. Give each student a copy of the Independent Birthday Graph on page 21. Have him or her transfer the information from the large Birthday Graph to the sheet; then answer the questions about the graph at the bottom of the sheet. Ask the student to complete the challenge on the back of the page.

14. Give students a copy of the Learning Calendar on page 22. The calendar has 20 spaces for writing. At the end of each day, have students write one positive thing they did or learned that day. Send the calendars home at the end of each month. This calendar helps students remember the days of the week and the months of the year, and also gives parents information about what students have learned each month.

15. At the end of each month, discuss all the special activities that happened during that month. Have each student use story paper to write about one of the special activities and then illustrate his or her story. Copy the cover on page 24 onto construction paper. Arrange all the monthly stories in order, add the cover and a construction paper back, and send the stories home at the end of the year. (**Alternative**: Using the pattern on page 23, create a one-page calendar that includes all of the school months and have students draw a picture representing a special activity that happened during each month in the correct space. Use the cover in the same way as above to make a book to send home at the end of the year.)

EXTENDING THE BOOK

1. To introduce the Author Study, challenge the students to find books in the library that are written or illustrated by Maurice Sendak. Do a search on the Internet using "Maurice Sendak" as a key term to find out more about the author and other books he has written and illustrated.

2. Use the recipe on page 25 to make chicken soup with your students.

3. While it is cooking, have students write the directions for the soup using transitional words, such as *first, second, then, next, last,* and *finally.* You may wish to use How to Prepare Chicken Soup on page 26 as an outline for the students.

4. Use the last page of the book, *Chicken Soup with Rice,* to extend an invitation to parents, another classroom, or faculty members to join your class for a hot cup of soup. Students will enjoy decorating the invitations with pictures of their favorite seasons.

5. Make special placemats for the occasion. Reproduce the pictures on pages 15–16 for each student. Have him or her color, cut out, and glue the pictures onto a colored sheet of 12" x 18" (30 cm x 46 cm) construction paper. Laminate the placemats before use.

Birthday Bulletin Board

Child's Picture

Happy Birthday _____

Birth Date _____

Picture Symbols

January
(observed 3ʳᵈ Monday in January)
Dr. Martin Luther King's Birthday

March
St. Patrick's Day

February
Valentine's Day

April
(observed 1ˢᵗ Sunday after first full
moon during Spring Equinox)
Easter

Birthday Bulletin Board *(cont.)*

Picture Symbols *(cont.)*

May
May Day

June
Flag Day

July
Independence Day

August
School Starts

September
(Sunday after Labor Day)
Grandparents Day

October
Halloween

November
Thanksgiving

December
Christmas

December
Hanukkah

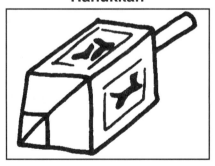

December
Kwanzaa

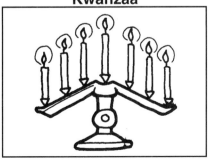

Rhyme Chimes

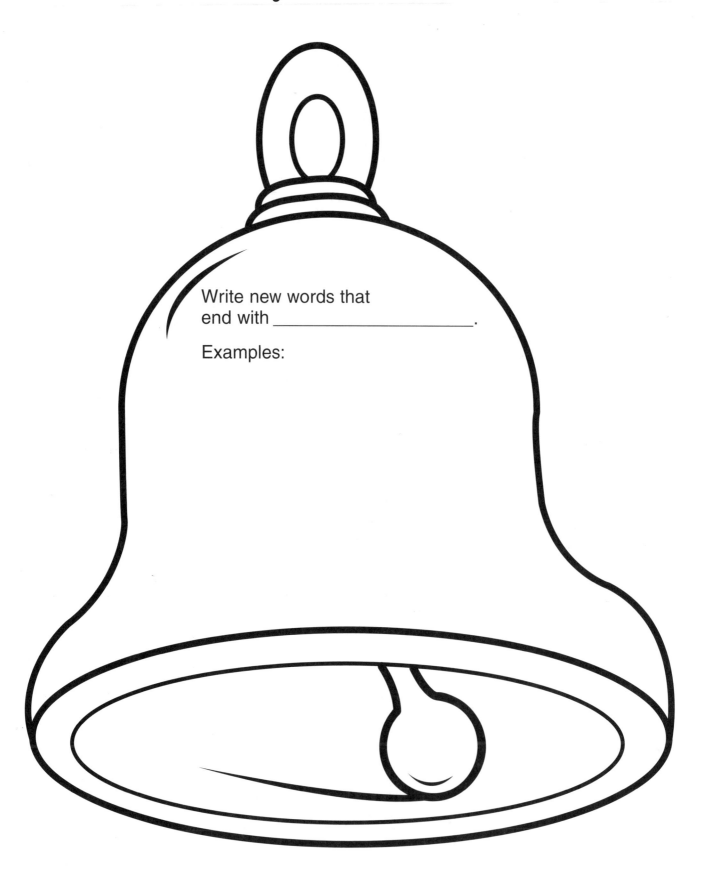

Write new words that
end with _____.

Examples:

Rhyme Chime Word Endings

(Word Families)

Examples of words and endings to use with the Rhyme Chimes activity.

ab	lab/jab
ad	sad/bad
ag	tag/nag
am	clam/slam
an	fan/man
ap	cap/slap
at	sat/cat
aw	law/saw
ay	day/may

ace	trace/space
ack	back/rack
ail	nail/frail
ain	chain/rain
air	chair/fair
ake	stake/rake
all	call/ball
and	sand/hand
ank	bank/tank
ark	mark/dark
ash	lash/cash
ate	skate/slate

able	cable/table
atch	match/scratch

ed	bed/fed
ee	bee/three
en	den/men
et	yet/set

ear	fear/year
eat	seat/meat
eed	feed/seed
eel	feel/wheel
eep	beep/peep
ell	fell/well
end	blend/spend
est	chest/pest

each	teach/reach

id	did/lid
ig	pig/dig
im	swim/him
in	win/tin
ip	whip/hip
it	sit/wit

ice	nice/rice
ick	quick/click
ide	side/ride
ill	pill/fill
ind	wind/bind
ine	fine/twine
ing	ring/cling
ink	stink/link

ight	light/sight

ob	mob/sob
od	nod/pod
og	dog/frog
op	top/stop
ot	rot/tot
ow	bow/show

oil	spoil/boil
oke	joke/stroke
old	cold/fold
ool	pool/school
oon	soon/moon
out	shout/about
own	frown/drown

ound	ground/sound

ug	dug/rug
um	gum/drum
un	run/bun
ut	hut/rut

ust	crust/must
ump	bump/lump

Rhyming Words

Write two rhyming words for each ending sound pattern.

at   _____   _____   an   _____   _____

ay   _____   _____   all   _____   _____

et   _____   _____   end   _____   _____

eed   _____   _____   each   _____   _____

id   _____   _____   ick   _____   _____

ing   _____   _____   ight   _____   _____

ob   _____   _____   old   _____   _____

ow   _____   _____   own   _____   _____

um   _____   _____   un   _____   _____

ust   _____   _____   ug   _____   _____

Challenge: Write a poem using at least four of the rhyming words on this page.

_____

_____

_____

Ordinal Number Pocket Chart
Month Pictures

January

February

March

April

May

June

Ordinal Number Pocket Chart *(cont.)*

July

August

September

October

November

December

agcust

Monthly Match

Write the months of the year in order. Then write the correct ordinal number beside each month. The first one has been completed for you.

Name of the Month	Ordinal Number for the Month
January	first—1st
Febuary	second—2nd
march	third—3rd
APRRl	fourth—4th
May	fith—5th
June	sixth—6th
July	seventh—7th
agsut August	eighth—8th

What is your favorite month of the year? _____

On the back of this page, draw a picture of something that happens in your favorite month.

ZOEY 2017

How Many Days?

Part I. Use the poem "Thirty Days Hath September" (below) and the word box to fill in the blanks. Some of the seasonal words will be used several times.

Thirty Days Hath September

Thirty days hath September, April, June, and November;
February has twenty-eight alone, All the rest have thirty-one,
Excepting leap year, that's the time, When February's days are twenty-nine.

winter	sixth	fall	eighth
thirty-one	summer	seventh	ninth
first	twenty-eight	second	fifth
eleventh	third	twenty-nine	thirty
spring	fourth	tenth	twelfth

January is the _____ month.

January is in the season of _____ .

January has _____ days.

February is the _____ month.

February is in the season of _____ .

February has _____ days.

Except when leap year comes, and that's the time

When February's days are _____ .

March is the _____ month.

March is in the season of _____ .

March has _____ days.

April is the _____ month.

April is in the season of _____ .

April has _____ days.

May is the _____ month.

May is in the season of _____ .

May has _____ days.

How Many Days? *(cont.)*

June is the _____ month.

June is in the season of _____ .

June has _____ days.

July is the _____ month.

July is in the season of _____ .

July has _____ days.

August is the _____ month.

August is in the season of _____ .

August has _____ days.

September is the _____ month.

September is in the season of _____ .

September has _____ days.

October is the _____ month.

October is in the season of _____ .

October has _____ days.

November is the _____ month.

November is in the season of _____ .

November has _____ days.

December is the _____ month.

December is in the season of _____ .

December has _____ days.

Part II. On another sheet of paper, write a story about your favorite month and season of the year. Illustrate your story. You may begin writing your story using the following:

My favorite month of the year is _____ in the season

of _____ because . . .

Chicken Soup with Rice

Birthday Poem

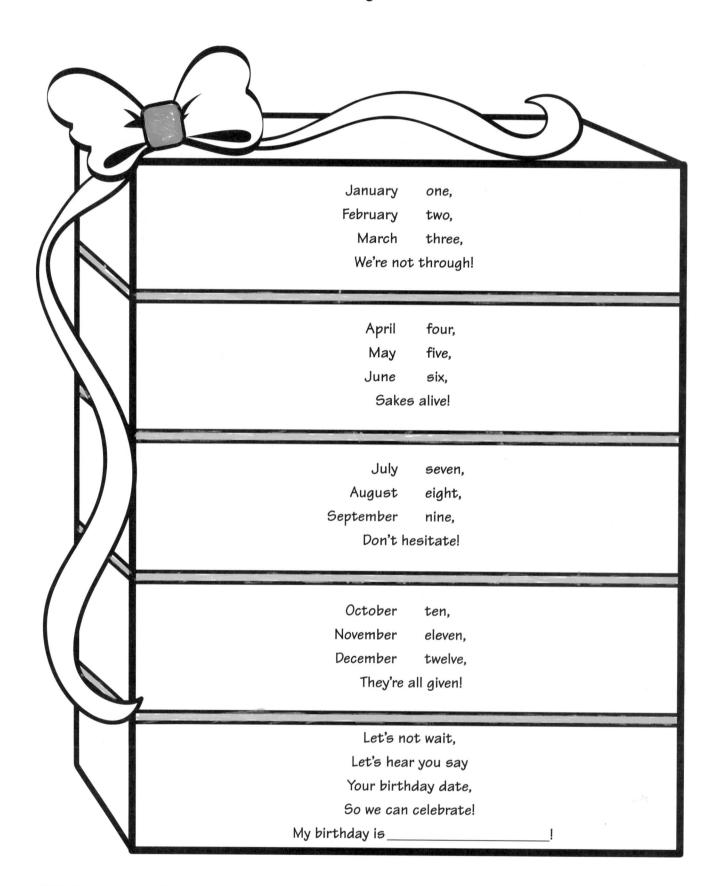

January   one,
February   two,
March   three,
We're not through!

April   four,
May   five,
June   six,
Sakes alive!

July   seven,
August   eight,
September nine,
Don't hesitate!

October   ten,
November   eleven,
December   twelve,
They're all given!

Let's not wait,
Let's hear you say
Your birthday date,
So we can celebrate!
My birthday is _____!

Independent Birthday Graph

Copy the information from the large Birthday Graph. Then, answer the questions at the bottom of the page.

Month	Number of Birthdays							
January								
February								
March								
April								
May								
June								
July	B	A	I L	EY				
August	Io	EY						
September	R							
October	BR	IA	NA	BA	RB	A RA		
November	BR	BR						
December								
	1	**2**	**3**	**4**	**5**	**6**	**7**	**8**

1. Which month (or months) has the most birthdays? _____

_____

2. Which month (or months) has the least birthdays? _____

_____

3. Write the name of each month that has the same amount of birthdays. _____

_____

4. How many birthdays are there on the Birthday Chart? _____

Challenge: Make five addition and five subtraction facts using the Independent Birthday Graph. (Example: How many birthdays are in May and July?)

Chicken Soup with Rice

Learning Calendar

This is the month of: _____.

Monday	Tuesday	Wednesday	Thursday	Friday

This Learning Calendar belongs to: _____.

School-Year Calendar

September	February
October	March
November	April
December	May
January	June

My
School
Year

By: _____

Chicken Soup Recipe

Use the recipe below to make chicken soup with your students.

Ingredients

- 4 boneless, skinless chicken breasts
- 2 chopped carrots
- 2 stalks chopped celery
- ½ bay leaf
- 1 small chopped onion

- 8 cups water
- 1 cup rice
- 1 small jar pimento
- salt/pepper to taste

Directions

Boil chicken, carrots, celery, bay leaf, and onion in 6 cups water until tender. Remove chicken and chop into small pieces. Add 2 cups water and bring to a boil. Add rice to soup mixture and cook until rice is tender. Add all the other ingredients, along with the chicken pieces, and simmer about 15 minutes. Add more water if needed. Remove bay leaf and serve with crackers.

Note: Check for any allergies before serving.

How to Prepare Chicken Soup

Today we made chicken soup.

First, _____

_____

_____

Second, _____

_____

_____

Next, _____

_____

_____

Then, _____

_____

_____

Last, _____

_____

_____

Finally, the soup was ready and now we will eat it. Yum! Yum!

The Apple Pie Tree

by Zoe Hall

Summary

"My sister and I have a tree that grows the best part of an apple pie." With that introduction, you can't resist the book The Apple Pie Tree. *This book takes children through the seasons from winter to fall as they watch an apple tree produce apples. At the same time, they watch a nest of baby robins develop and grow. The brightly colored pictures, created from paint and found-paper collage, offer children a vivid picture of nature and its wonder.*

The outline below is a suggested plan for using the variety of activities presented in this unit. You should adapt these ideas to fit your classroom situation.

Sample Plan

Day 1

- Introduce the four seasons using Why Do We Have Seasons? (pages 31–32), Orbital Seasons (pages 33–34), and Earth's Axis (page 35).
- Play Seasonal Line Up activity every day (see page 30, #13).
- Read *The Apple Pie Tree.*
- Complete the Season Chart (page 28, #1).
- Do Seasonal Patterned Writing (page 36).
- Create the Seasonal Book (page 29, #6).
- Write the "Sense"-sational Seasonal Poems (page 51).

Day 2

- Read *The Apple Pie Tree.*
- Complete the open-ended writing activity, My Favorite Season (page 29, #7).
- Create the My Favorite Season Pictograph (page 37).
- Complete the Individual Season Pictograph (page 38).
- Write the "Sense"-sational Seasonal Poems (page 51).

Day 3

- Read *The Apple Pie Tree.*
- Create the Seasonal Apple Tree Collages (pages 39–43).
- Prepare the leaves for Leaf Rubbings (see page 44).
- Write the "Sense"-sational Poems (page 51).

Day 4

- Read *The Apple Pie Tree.*
- Create the Leaf Rubbings (pages 44–49).
- Create the Seasonal Stained Glass Leaves (page 50).
- Write the "Sense"-sational Poems (page 51).

Day 5

- Do the Seasonal Sentence Match (pages 52–53).
- Complete Extending the Book activities (pages 30, 54–59).
- Make Apple Pies and hold an Apple Pie Party (page 30, #5 and #6).

Overview of Activities

SETTING THE STAGE

1. Prepare a Season Chart on a large sheet of bulletin-board paper. Write the name of each season as a heading; the rest of the chart will be completed during the activity. (See Appendix: Season Chart.)

2. Prepare the large My Favorite Season Pictograph on a sheet of poster board. (See page 37 for example of pictograph.)

3. All About Trees: Nature has created many different kinds of trees, but needle-leaf trees and broad-leaf trees are the two most common varieties. Needle-leaf trees, or evergreens, can stand harsh cold or burning sun and their leaves still stay green. Broad-leaf trees lose their leaves in winter and are dormant or resting until spring. These are known as deciduous trees. Deciduous trees grow best in climates that have clearly defined seasons so that the tree can rest in winter. Apple trees are deciduous trees. An apple tree produces apples from age 5–40 years. There are thousands of different kinds of apples and over 100 are grown commercially in the United States. Apples can be yellow, red, or green in color. The science of apple growing is called *pomology* because *pomme* is the French word for "apple."

4. Why Leaves Change Colors: Leaves are very important to a tree. The leaves make a kind of sugar that the tree uses for food. In the fall, there are not as many hours of daylight and the tree begins to get ready to rest for the winter. It does not need as much food and does not need its leaves anymore. As the leaves die and begin to separate from the tree, they get less water, and without bright sunlight and water, leaves cannot make chlorophyll (the natural green coloring that keeps them green). The green leaf color begins to fade and new colors, which have been in the leaf all along, show through. Bright days and cool nights bring out the beautiful leaves' fall colors of red, orange, yellow, and brown.

ENJOYING THE BOOK

1. Spring, summer, fall, and winter are the seasons that divide the year. Earth's movement around the sun and the tilt of Earth's axis cause the seasonal changes. Introduce the seasons by reading Why Do We Have Seasons? (pages 31–32) and completing Orbital Seasons (pages 33–34).

2. Use page 35 to demonstrate how Earth's axis contributes to the changing of the seasons.

3. Introduce the book *The Apple Pie Tree* to the students. Read the title and the name of the author and illustrator. Read the book through once for enjoyment, showing the pictures after you read each page. As you read the book again, emphasize the seasonal changes by discussing the illustrations. Ask students to notice the weather, the way the trees look, how the children are dressed, and how the baby birds change during the different seasons.

4. Use the prepared Season Chart to review the four seasons with the students. Remind students about clothing, weather, and activities they do during the different seasons and list them on the chart. Be sure to list the months that occur in each season. Post the chart in an area that is visible to all students to use with the Seasonal Patterned Writing activity (page 29).

Overview of Activities *(cont.)*

ENJOYING THE BOOK *(cont.)*

5. Copy the Seasonal Patterned Writing activity (page 36) for each student. Demonstrate how to use the Season Chart (page 28) to fill in the blanks on the page. Help the students edit the paper to check for errors because they will use the writing in the next activity, Seasonal Book.

6. To complete the Seasonal Book activity, give each student four sheets of 8½" x 11" (22 cm x 28 cm) writing paper with a drawing area at the top and one sheet of 8½" x 11" (22 cm x 28 cm) white paper to use as a title page. Have him or her use the Seasonal Patterned Writing activity to copy one poem onto each of the four pages; then illustrate the poem in the drawing area. Guide the student to create a title page on the white paper using his or her name as author and illustrator. If you want to add a publisher, use "Published by: Mr. or Mrs. _____ class." Fold a sheet of 11" x 17" (28 cm x 43 cm) colored construction paper in half. Place the title page and four poem sheets between the folded paper and staple on the fold to create a book. Have the student write a title on the cover and draw seasonal pictures on it to complete the book.

7. Have the students complete an open-ended writing assignment beginning with "My Favorite Season is _____because _____." Tell them to write a paragraph with a main idea sentence and at least three supporting sentences telling why the season they chose is their favorite. They should also complete the paragraph by restating the main idea. This activity should be adapted for younger students who may only be able to write one or two reasons.

8. Copy the Seasonal Symbols from page 37 to match the favorite season in the students' writing (above). Use the prepared My Favorite Season Pictograph (see page 28) for this activity. Have each student color and cut out the symbol that represents his or her favorite season and glue it to the pictograph. Discuss the pictograph in detail; then extend the activity by having students transfer the pictograph to the Individual Season Pictograph (page 38). Finally, have the students answer the related questions.

9. Tell the students that Shari Halpern, the illustrator of *The Apple Pie Tree*, created the pictures using a collage technique. They can make pictures using the same kind of collage art. Copy the four Seasonal Apple Tree Pictures (pages 40–43) onto white construction paper. You may choose to have each student make all four seasonal trees, or divide the students into groups of four and have each group make a different Seasonal Apple Tree Collage. If each student makes all four trees, this activity should be divided into four days. The directions for making the four different trees are on page 39.

10. Discuss the reason the leaves change colors with students using information from Why Leaves Change Colors (page 28, #4). Students enjoy making leaf rubbings, but sometimes leaves are not available or they are too dry or wet to be used to make rubbings. Use the leaf patterns and directions on pages 44–49 to make Leaf Rubbings during any season of the year. Use the directions on page 50 and the large leaf patterns (pages 45–49) to make Seasonal Stained Glass Leaves for windows or room decorations.

Overview of Activities *(cont.)*

ENJOYING THE BOOK *(cont.)*

11. Introduce poetry writing to students and allow them to create their own "Sense"-sational poems. (See directions on page 51.)

12. To check students' knowledge of the seasonal concept, assign Seasonal Sentence Match (pages 52–53) as an independent activity.

13. Play Seasonal Line Up with your students. When it's time to line up for lunch or other activities, choose a season and have students earn a place in line by giving a vocabulary word that fits the season. Extend the activity using holidays or any concept that is being taught.

EXTENDING THE BOOK

1. There are several legends about how the star got inside an apple. Read the short story, "A Special Star," on page 54 to the students. After reading the story, cut an apple in half horizontally to reveal the five-pointed star inside. Have the students write what happened at the beginning, middle, and end of the story using a Fold Book. (See directions on page 55.)

2. Use the Apple Adventure activities on pages 56–58 for apple art, apple science, apple math, and apple writing (with Bloom's Taxonomy).

3. Bring a red, a green, and a yellow apple, along with applesauce, apple pie, apple butter, and apple juice to share with the students. Discuss the different kinds of trees using All About Trees (page 28, #3). Show the students the different apples and ask them to describe how the apples look using descriptive words, such as color. Pass the apples around and allow them to describe how the apples feel and smell. List the descriptive words on a chart. Tell the students that they can use their senses to describe other things that are made from apples. Give each student a small sample of each of the apple products you brought. Use Apple Senses (page 59) to have students describe the way each apple product looks, feels, smells, and tastes using one word.

4. During the week that *The Apple Pie Tree* activities are taking place, ask parents to provide different kinds of apple snacks each day for the students.

5. On the last page of *The Apple Pie Tree*, an apple pie recipe is included. Elicit help from parents to make apple pies with the students.

6. Plan an Apple Pie Party to share the apple pies with parents, the principal, staff members, or other students. Check for allergies before serving. During the party, display all of the projects from *The Apple Pie Tree* unit, and have students read the book to their guests.

Why Do We Have Seasons?

Spring, summer, fall, and winter are the seasons that divide the year. Earth's orbit, or movement around the sun, and the tilt of Earth's axis cause the seasonal changes. As the seasons change, temperature, weather, and the length of daylight also change.

The Earth orbits around the sun in an *ellipse*. An ellipse is a slightly flattened circle.

Earth makes one full orbit around the sun each year (365 days). Because of the elliptical orbit, Earth travels closest to the sun in January and moves farthest away from the sun in July.

Earth does not sit in a straight up-and-down position. It is tipped 23.5° on what is known as an *axis*, the imaginary line that runs from the North Pole to the South Pole. The direction of Earth's tilt changes in relation to the sun, giving the northern and southern halves of Earth differing amounts of sunlight during the year.

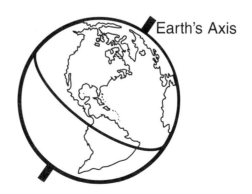

Why Do We Have Seasons? *(cont.)*

Earth is divided in half by an imaginary line called the *equator*. The top, northern half is called the northern hemisphere and the bottom, southern half is called the southern hemisphere.

When the northern hemisphere is tipped toward the sun, that half has summer and the southern hemisphere has winter. When Earth tips in the other direction, the southern hemisphere has summer and the northern hemisphere has winter. Twice during the year, the heat from the sun is about equal on both halves of Earth. Then one half has spring and the other half has fall.

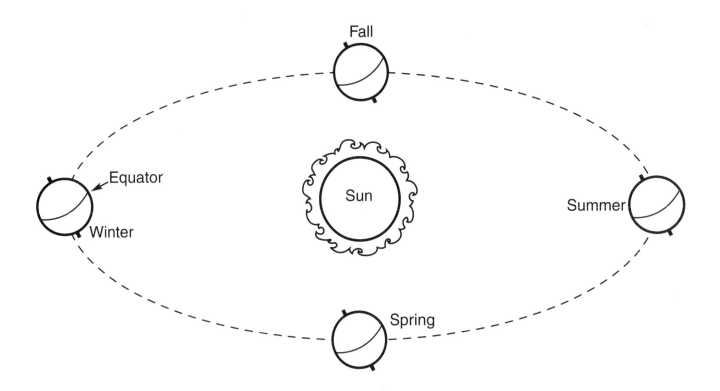

Seasons in the Northern Hemisphere

The seasons of spring, summer, fall, and winter are based on temperature and weather and are known as *climatic seasons*. Some regions on Earth do not have all four climatic seasons. In some parts of the world, temperatures change very little and so there are no seasonal changes.

Orbital Seasons

Materials:

- chalk
- sheet of yellow poster board
- 4 copies of Earth (page 34)
- large ball (e.g., a beach ball)

Directions:

Cut the yellow poster board into a circle to represent the sun. Draw a black line around the center of the ball to represent the equator. Clear the center of the classroom and use chalk to draw a very large ellipse on the floor. Place the sun pattern in the center of the ellipse. Place the earth patterns in position for spring, summer, fall, and winter, as shown here.

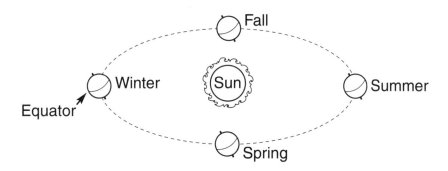

Seasons in the Northern Hemisphere

Rotating

Demonstrate the rotating earth by spinning the ball around and around. Explain to the students that Earth turns around one time every 24 hours, making one day and one night.

Revolving

Spin the ball as you follow the elliptical orbit to demonstrate Earth as it revolves around the sun.

Changing Seasons

Remind students that Earth doesn't sit straight up and down as it spins, but tilts sideways to create the seasons. Follow the path around the ellipse again, stopping at each picture of the earth. Pick up the picture and point out the tilt of the axis, the equator, and the northern and southern hemisphere. Ask, "What part of the world is having spring (or summer, fall, winter)?" Remind students about the opposite seasons of the northern and southern hemispheres.

Rotating and Revolving Fun

Choose a child to represent the earth. Demonstrate Earth's rotation and the way it revolves around the sun by having a child turn around and around as he or she follows the elliptical orbit.

Orbital Seasons *(cont.)*

Earth

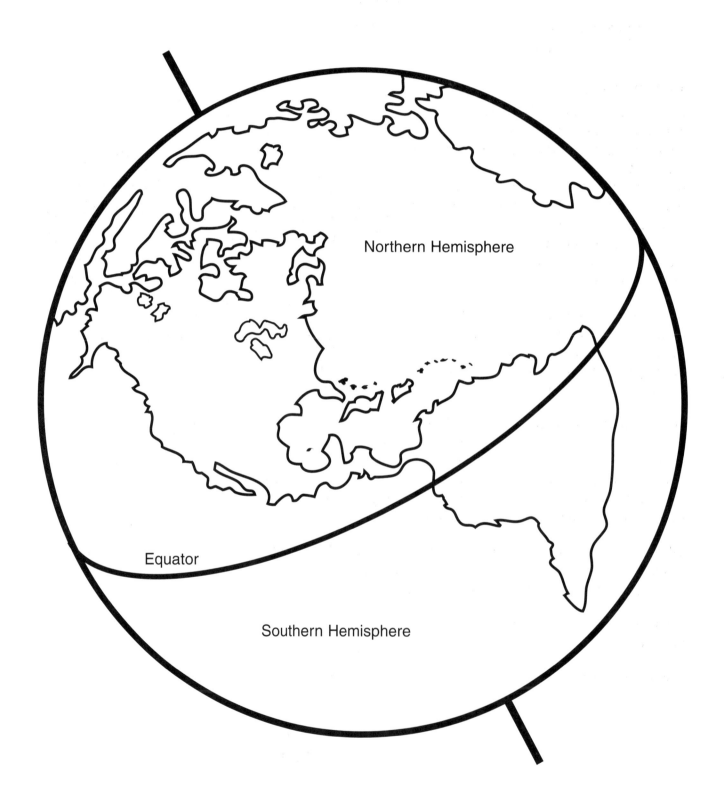

Northern Hemisphere

Equator

Southern Hemisphere

34

Earth's Axis

Materials:

- orange
- sharpened pencil
- black permanent marker
- flashlight
- straight pin

Directions:

Push the pencil through the center of the orange to represent Earth's axis. Draw a line around the center of the orange to represent the equator. Mark the top and bottom of the orange with an **N** to represent "north" and an **S** to represent "south." Push the straight pin into the orange to represent where the students are located. Explain each representation as you prepare the orange for the experiment.

Make sure the students understand that the representations are all imaginary and that Earth does not really have anything like a pencil going through its center. Earth spins as if there is something running through it.

Tell the students that the flashlight will represent the sun. Darken the room and have someone shine the flashlight on the orange. Turn the orange on its axis with the pencil straight up and down and move around the sun in a wide circle while rotating the pencil/axis. Point out that Earth makes one full rotation to create a day and night and makes one full revolution around the sun each year. During that year, there will be four seasonal changes in most places on Earth. Point out that if Earth stayed in the straight position, there would be no seasonal changes.

Tilt the pencil/axis so that the north is away from the sun and explain that in this position, the north would have winter and the south would have summer. Reverse the position to show the opposite and then explain how spring and fall occur.

Locate the pin and discuss the different seasonal changes as Earth rotates and revolves around the sun.

Allow the students time for hands-on experimentation with the orange to complete the lesson.

Seasonal Patterned Writing

Spring

Spring is the months of March, April, and May.

Spring is _____.

Spring is _____.

Spring is _____.

Spring.

Summer

Summer is the months of June, July, and August.

Summer is _____.

Summer is _____.

Summer is _____.

Summer.

Fall

Fall is the months of September, October, and November.

Fall is _____.

Fall is _____.

Fall is _____.

Fall.

Winter

Winter is the months of December, January, and February.

Winter is _____.

Winter is _____.

Winter is _____.

Winter.

My Favorite Season Pictograph

Directions: Have each student color a seasonal symbol below to represent his or her favorite season.

Seasonal Symbols

Spring

Fall
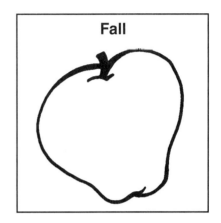

Summer

Winter

Our Favorite Seasons

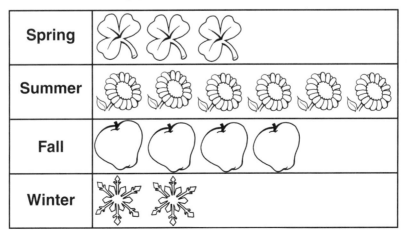

Individual Season Pictograph

Directions: Draw the seasonal symbols on the graph below to match the pictograph made by the class. Answer the questions about the pictograph.

Spring	
Summer	
Fall	
Winter	

1. How many children like ❀ best? _____

2. How many children like ❀ best? _____

3. How many children like 🍎 best? _____

4. How many children like ❄ best? _____

5. Which season do the most children like? _____

6. Which season do the least children like? _____

Directions for the Seasonal Apple Tree Collages

Copy the Seasonal Apple Tree Pictures (pages 40–43) onto white construction paper for durability. After the collages are completed, lay them on a flat surface to dry for several hours. All of the tree trunks, the leaves, and grass should be colored before beginning the following directions.

Spring Materials:
- Spring Apple Tree Picture
- pink tissue paper
- scissors
- crayons
- glue

Directions for Making the Spring Apple Tree Collage:
Cut the tissue paper into small 1" (2.5 cm) squares. Put a square on the eraser end of a pencil and twist it around to make a pink flower. Glue the tissue paper atop the flowers on the spring apple tree to create apple blossoms.

Summer Materials:
- Summer Apple Tree Picture
- red tissue paper
- crayons
- scissors
- glue

Directions for Making the Summer Apple Tree Collage:
Cut the tissue paper into small 2" or 3" (5 cm or 8 cm) squares. Roll the tissue squares into small balls; then glue the balls atop the apples on the summer tree to create apples.

Fall Materials:
- Fall Apple Tree Picture
- crayons
- glue
- red, green, orange, yellow, and brown construction paper

Directions for Making the Fall Apple Tree Collage:
Tear off tiny pieces of different colored construction paper, about the size of the leaves on the fall tree, and glue the pieces atop the leaves on the tree. Make sure the pieces overlap to cover all the leaves.

Winter Materials:
- Winter Apple Tree Picture
- white cotton balls
- crayons
- glue

Directions for Making the Winter Apple Tree Collage:
Tear off tiny pieces of the cotton balls and roll them to make tiny balls. Glue the balls atop the snow on the picture.

Seasonal Apple Tree Pictures

Spring Apple Tree

40

Seasonal Apple Tree Pictures *(cont.)*

Summer Apple Tree

Seasonal Apple Tree Pictures *(cont.)*

Fall Apple Tree

Seasonal Apple Tree Pictures *(cont.)*

Winter Apple Tree

Leaf Rubbings

Materials:

- copies of Leaf Patterns on pages 45–49 (at least 1 for each student)
- white glue

Directions for Preparing for Leaf Rubbings:

Teachers of younger children may prefer to prepare several leaf patterns without the assistance of students; then let the students make the rubbings.

Have the students put a thin, unbroken line of glue along all of the lines on the leaf pattern. Make sure they follow the lines exactly. The stem line should be slightly thicker than the other lines.

Allow the leaves to dry on a flat surface for several hours or overnight. Be careful when moving the patterns before the glue is dry because the glue will run.

Materials:

- leaf patterns traced with glue (see Preparation for Leaf Rubbings)
- used crayons (bright colors)
- white paper
- tape
- scissors

Directions for Making Leaf Rubbings:

1. Peel the paper off the crayons. Have the students use bright colored crayons to show the leaves during different seasons of the year.

2. Lay the leaf pattern on a flat table with the glue side up.

3. Place a sheet of white paper on top of the leaf pattern. Tape both papers to the table to keep them from moving.

4. Using the side of a crayon, rub across the entire white surface. The leaf pattern will transfer to the white paper. Allow students to exchange patterns and make new leaves.

5. Cut the leaves out. Have students compare the rubbings of the different leaves, and discuss why the leaves are shaped differently.

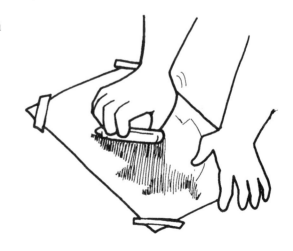

Leaf Patterns

Holly Leaf Pattern

Leaf Patterns *(cont.)*

Maple Leaf Pattern

Leaf Patterns *(cont.)*

Tulip Tree Leaf Pattern

Leaf Patterns *(cont.)*

Oak Leaf Pattern

Leaf Patterns *(cont.)*

Elm Leaf Pattern

Seasonal Stained Glass Leaves

Materials:

- laminating film (that has not been run through the laminator)
- bright colored crayons
- iron (set on medium)
- crayon sharpeners
- copies of Leaf Patterns on pages 45–49 (one pattern for each student)

Directions:

1. Have students sharpen crayons and collect the shavings.

2. Fold a piece of laminating film in half to fit the size of the leaf pattern. Sprinkle crayon shavings between the fold in the laminating film.

3. Iron over the laminating film until all the crayon shavings are melted and the film is fused together. (**Safety Note:** Teacher or another adult will need to carefully monitor this step.)

4. Tape the leaf pattern on top of the fused laminating film and cut out the leaf pattern. Hang the leaves in the window to create a stained glass effect.

"Sense"-sational Seasonal Poems

Have the students use their senses during a discussion of the four seasons. Bring in several pictures for each season. Select a season and show its pictures, one at a time. Discuss the details in the pictures. Emphasize the holidays, weather, and clothing for that season. Ask the students what they might hear, see, smell, taste, feel, or touch during that season. List the sense words on a chart. Show each picture and continue the discussion. This activity should be divided into four days, featuring one season per day.

Have the students use the form below as a prewriting activity before writing a poem.
(**Note**: Make sure the students understand that not all poetry has to rhyme. Explain that it only has to have a sense of pattern, sound, and regular rhythm to be considered poetry.)

Spring Example:

In the spring, I can hear _____.

In the spring, I can smell_____.

In the spring, I can see _____.

In the spring, I can taste _____.

In the spring, I can feel _____.

In the spring, I can touch _____.

But I cannot see _____.

In the spring, I can hear <u>birds singing</u>.

In the spring, I can smell <u>pretty flowers</u>.

In the spring, I can see <u>green trees</u>.

In the spring, I can taste <u>hot dogs</u>.

In the spring, I can feel <u>warm breezes</u>.

In the spring, I can touch <u>soft blossoms</u>.

But I cannot see <u>snow falling</u>.

Spring

Spring is . . .

birds singing

pretty flowers

green trees

hot dogs

warm breezes

soft blossoms

but not snow falling.

Seasonal Sentence Match

Materials:

- Seasonal scenes and sentences from this page and page 53
- construction paper   • scissors   • glue

Directions:

Color and cut out the scenes and glue them onto construction paper. Cut out and glue the correct seasonal sentence under the matching scene.

In spring, it is time to plant seeds.
They will grow into pretty flowers.

In fall, colorful leaves drop to the ground. It is time to rake.

In summer, it is very hot. Playing in the sand and swimming is fun.

In winter, it is cold and the snow falls. It's time to build a snowman.

Spring

Seasonal Sentence Match *(cont.)*

Summer

Fall

Winter

A Special Star

Once upon a time, there was a tiny brown seed hidden deep in the warm soil. One day the tiny seed burst open. A small green stem pushed its way out of the ground, and discovered a beautiful new world. The tiny seed had grown into a small apple tree. The apple tree thought the daytime with its bright, warm sunshine was a wonderful place. But the nighttime with the dark sky and canopy of stars was the most beautiful to her. She wished with all her heart that she could have just one small star for her very own.

The fairy queen heard the tiny tree's wish and told her that if she worked hard to grow strong and healthy, her wish would be granted. The apple tree did just that! One spring day, when she was about five years old, she found her branches covered with beautiful pink blossoms. When her blossoms dropped off, she had small baby seeds that someday would grow into apple trees just like her.

She was so happy, loving and caring for her baby seeds that she forgot all about her wish. But the fairy queen had not forgotten. One day the fairy queen told the apple tree that she had earned her wish and she would make a crown of stars for the apple tree.

The tree told the fairy to give the stars to her baby seeds instead. And to this day, every apple has a star in its heart!

Fold Book

Beginning, Middle, End

Fold books give students a clearly defined work area for writing and illustrating.

① Fold a long sheet of white paper into three sections, as you would fold a letter before putting it into an envelope (a). With the paper still folded, fold it in half again and crease the fold lines (b). When the paper is opened, it should have six spaces for writing and illustrations.

Fold 1   Fold 2

Fold 3

ⓐ

ⓑ

② Tell the students to each place the paper in front of them so there are three spaces at the top and three spaces at the bottom. Have them write what happened at the beginning of the story in the first space on the bottom of the papers, what happened in the middle in the second space on the bottom, and what happened at the end of the story in the last space on the bottom (see diagram below).

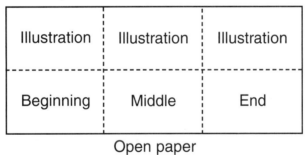

Illustration	Illustration	Illustration
Beginning	Middle	End

Open paper

The students illustrate their stories in the three spaces above their writing at the top of the paper.

③ After the writing and the illustrations are completed, with the paper still in the same position, have students fold the last section over toward the left. Then have them fold the first section over toward the right and crease the fold to create the front of the fold book. Finally, have them write the titles on the top space and their names on the bottom space as shown.

Title

Name

Closed paper

Apple Adventures
Art Activities

The following activities can be used anytime to extend *The Apple Pie Tree* unit.

Paint an Apple Tree

Materials:

- brown construction paper
- sheets of white construction paper
- tempera paint (red, yellow, light and dark green)
- scissors
- glue
- paintbrushes

Directions:

Cut brown construction paper in the shape of a tree trunk. Glue the trunk onto a sheet of white construction paper. Use dark green tempera paint to paint the top of the tree. After the tree is dry, dip fingertips into red, yellow, or light green paint and print apples on the tree.

Paper Bag Apple

Materials:

- small lunch bags
- newspaper for stuffing sacks
- green construction paper
- red, green, and yellow tempera paint
- paintbrushes
- glue
- tape
- scissors

Directions:

Cut apple leaves from green construction paper. Stuff newspaper into a lunch bag until it is a little over half full. Tightly twist the remainder of the bag to form the apple stem. Tape the stem to hold it in place and close the sack. Squeeze and shape the bag until it is fairly round. Paint the bag using one of the colors of an apple. When dry, glue the leaves onto the paper bag apple.

Apple Creatures/Apple Santa

Materials:

- apples (1 for each child)
- toothpicks
- an assortment of soft candy
- large and small gumdrops
- large and small marshmallows

Directions:

Have students position the toothpicks on the apple as arms, legs, and a head. Use large marshmallows for the head, arms, and legs; then use the candy to create facial features for the apple creature.

Use red apples to make the Apple Santa in the same way. Add large gumdrops on top of the marshmallow head and small gumdrops on the ends of arms and legs. Use an assortment of small candies for eyes, nose, and a mouth. (The apples will stay fresh for only two to three days, so plan to eat them within that time period.)

Apple Adventures *(cont.)*

Math/Science Activities

Apple Water Content

Materials:

- apple slices (1 slice for each student)
- small scale that will measure ounces
- yarn
- paper and pencil

Directions:

A full-grown apple tree uses 4 gallons of water an hour, or 96 gallons a day. This experiment focuses on water weight.

Cut the apples into four quarters. Give each student a slice of apple and a piece of yarn. Each student will tie the piece of yarn around the slice, weigh the slice, and record the weight. Then the slices should be hung to dry. Students can weigh the slices every other day and record the weight difference. As the apples dry and lose water, the weight decreases.

Apple Measure

Materials:

- apple
- yarn
- markers (four different colors)
- ruler

Directions:

Wrap a piece of yarn around the top section of an apple. Mark the point where the string meets using a colored marker. (Use a different colored marker to mark the yarn for each measurement.) Lay the yarn over a ruler and record the measurement for circumference. Follow the same procedure to measure the middle and bottom of the apple.

Cut the apple in half horizontally. Lay the string across the inside of the cut apple to measure the diameter. Use the ruler in the same way to record the apple's diameter.

Apple Adventures *(cont.)*

Language Art Activities

Apple Book

Materials:
- 8½" x 14" (22 cm x 35 cm, legal size) sheet of white paper, folded in half
- crayons and pencils

This activity is designed to teach students to follow directions. They should each make a small book using a sample supplied by the teacher, copy the writing in the book, and then illustrate the book according to the writing on each page.

Teacher Sample: Fold a legal size sheet of paper in half to make a small four-page book. Write "Apples" on the front as a title.

Write the following on the three remaining pages:

1. This apple is red.   2. This apple is green.   3. This apple is yellow.

Put the sample book, folded paper, crayons, and pencils at a center. Have each student copy the teacher-made book, draw an apple on each page, and color the apple according to the color stated on that page. Then have them each decorate the front of the book with more apple illustrations and add their names to complete the activity.

Writing with Bloom's Taxonomy

To assess student learning at the different levels of Bloom's Taxonomy, use the following writing activities. For student knowledge to be internalized, they must be able to function at the higher levels of application.

Bloom's Taxonomy includes:

1. **Knowledge**
   - Make a list of several uses for apples. Share your ideas with other students.
2. **Comprehension**
   - Read the book, *Johnny Appleseed*. Retell the story to a group of younger students.
3. **Application**
   - Make applesauce. Write a short summary describing the steps you used to make it.
4. **Analysis**
   - Write a paragraph comparing and contrasting an apple with a grapefruit or another fruit.
5. **Synthesis**
   - Brainstorm a list of words describing apples. Use as many of the words as possible to write an original poem.
   - Write a story using one of the following titles (or an original title):
      The Giant Green Apple; The Apple Twins; Suzy, the Apple Worm
6. **Evaluation**
   - Write a paragraph describing how you would feel if you were an apple or a worm living inside an apple.

Apple Senses

After sampling the five apple products, list words in the boxes to describe how each apple product looks, feels, smells, and tastes.

Product	Looks	Feels	Smells	Tastes
Apple				
Applesauce				
Apple Pie				
Apple Butter				
Apple Juice				

Language Connections

The Spanish language has five basic vowel sounds represented by the same vowels (a, e, i, o, u) as those of the English language. Use the vowel chart below to help students learn the days of the week, the months, and the seasons in Spanish.

Spanish Vowel Pronunciation					
A a	as in *father*	/ah	O o	as in *owe*	/long o
E e	as in *they*	/long a	U oo	as in *moon*	/oo
I i	as in *machine*	/long e			

Days of the Week

Sunday . . . . *domingo*
Monday . . . . *lunes*
Tuesday . . . . *martes*
Wednesday . . . . *mi'ercoles*
Thursday . . . . *jueves*
Friday . . . . *viernes*
Saturday . . . . *sabado*

Seasons

spring . . . . *la primavera*
summer . . . . *el verano*
fall . . . . *el otoño*
winter . . . . *el invierno*

Months

January . . . . *enero*
February . . . . *febrero*
March . . . . *marzo*
April . . . . *abril*
May . . . . *mayo*
June . . . . *junio*

July . . . . *julio*
August . . . . *agosto*
September . . . . *septiembre*
October . . . . *octubre*
November . . . . *noviembre*
December . . . . *diciembre*

--- Just for Fun ---

Spanish: En America del Norte, la primavera empieza en marzo.

English: In North America, spring begins in March.

Spanish: En America del Sur, la primavera empieza en septiembre.

English: In South America, spring begins in September.

Seasonal Scavenger Hunt

This scavenger hunt can be used during any season. Before going on the hunt, discuss the different things that might be found in the current season. Caution students not to pick up living creatures, such as spiders and insects that might sting or bite them. Living things can be observed with the magnifying glasses, but should not be collected.

Materials:

- magnifying glasses (1 for each student)
- small paper bags (1 for each student)

Directions for Seasonal Scavenger Hunt:

Give each student a paper bag and a magnifying glass. Walk around the schoolyard or a park and have each student collect five different things that show signs of the season and place the items in his or her bag.

Scavenger Hunt Write Along

Materials:

- chart paper
- different colored markers
- story writing paper with illustration section (1 for each student)
- pencils
- crayons

Directions for Scavenger Hunt Write Along:

After the scavenger hunt, have the students sit on the floor around a chart. Ask each student to choose one thing he or she collected. Have him or her describe the chosen object and dictate a sentence about the item for the teacher to write on the chart. The teacher should use a different color for each statement and the child's name. For example, the teacher may write:

Johnny said, "I found a red leaf for fall."

After everyone has had a turn, give each student story writing paper to copy the sentence that he or she dictated; then ask eack student to draw a picture of the found item on the illustration section of the paper. (The item can be attached to the paper if it is not too large.)

Language Arts

Word Find

```
D Y A D S R U H T A
M A R F A L L A S M
W D U O T D E P A O
F S A G W N F R T N
Y E S J U L Y I U T
A N K J L S M L R H
D D Y A M X T R D S
N E G N I R P S A E
U W T U E S D A Y A
S U M A R C H I G S
J A O R E T N I W O
O K T Y A D S E N N
O R E B M E V O N S
P C E F R I D A Y N
R S T Y A D N O M M
T U N O V E V B E R
N D A Y B I J Y D E
S Y A D S E N D E B
F E B R U A R Y C M
R C P B M A Z W E E
G A H T M J X I M T
S R E P E U N M B P
U V W Y R N U O E E
G D B A U E B I R S
```

APRIL	AUGUST	OCTOBER	SUNDAY
WINTER	JANUARY	SATURDAY	MAY
SEPTEMBER	MONDAY	SPRING	THURSDAY
FRIDAY	FEBRUARY	JUNE	NOVEMBER
WEDNESDAY	MARCH	TUESDAY	JULY
DECEMBER	SUMMER	FALL	MONTHS
DAYS	YEAR	SEASONS	

Word Scramble

Unscramble the words to spell a day of the week, month, or season. Remember to capitalize days of the week and months of the year.

Days of the Week

riayfd   _____

atsdyrau   _____

hurtsady   _____

tedusay   _____

nadmyo   _____

yadnsewde   _____

nsduay   _____

Seasons

lalf   _____

treinw   _____

mreusm   _____

rspngi   _____

Months

lyju	_____	usutag	_____
amhrc	_____	recdmebe	_____
aym	_____	etmeseprb	_____
rbeonvem	_____	jnaauyr	_____
eoctbor	_____	enju	_____
palri	_____	yeafrubr	_____

Months Crossword Puzzle

Across

2. The first month of spring is _____.
4. The first month of summer is _____.
5. The month before May is _____.
6. Thanksgiving comes in _____.
10. The first month of fall is _____.
11. The eighth month of the year is _____.

Down

1. The first month of the year is _____.
3. The last month of the year is _____.
4. Firecrackers explode on the Fourth of _____.
7. Halloween comes in _____.
8. April showers bring _____ flowers.
9. Valentine's Day is in _____.

Quick Check

1. There are _____ days in a week.

2. There are _____ seasons in a year.

3. There are _____ months in a year.

4. The days of the week in correct order are:

   1._____   5._____

   2._____   6._____

   3._____   7._____

   4._____

5. The seasons of the year are:

   _____   _____

   _____   _____

6. The three winter months are:

   _____   _____

   _____

7. The two months after March are:

   _____   _____

   _____

8. The three fall months are:

   _____   _____

   _____

9. The two months before August are:

   _____   _____

Holiday Math Wizard

Math Wizard is an easy way to learn how to solve word problems at an early age. Sample problems featuring favorite holidays from each month are listed on pages 67–68. The simple pictures can be used as illustrations for the word problems. Change the numbers to make new problems using the same pictures, or use new pictures to solve math problems in the textbook.

Materials (for each student):

- 2 sheets of 8½" x 14" (22 cm x 35 cm) paper
- pencil
- crayons

Directions for Holiday Math Wizard:

Begin by teaching students to identify math problems as addition or subtraction. Use the clue words "how many in all" and "how many are left." Next, teach how to fold the paper in half and in three parts. Write a math word problem on the board. Have the students identify the problem as addition or subtraction. Model solving the problem on the board using the directions below. Have students copy the problem from the board onto their papers until they understand the procedure.

Addition

For addition problems, have students fold their papers in three parts; then open them so that there are three work areas. They should put a plus (+) sign on the first fold and an equal (=) sign on the second fold. Then students write the problem at the top of their papers in number sentence form as shown below. Finally, they illustrate the addition problems.

Problem: *Spring is here! There are 2 birds in a tree. Then 3 more come. How many birds in all?*

Subtraction

For subtraction problems, have students fold their papers in half; then open them so that there are two working areas. They should put an equal (=) sign on the fold line. Then students write the problem in number sentence form at the top of the paper. Finally, students draw the pictures for the first number in the problem and cross out the number that should be subtracted as shown below.

Problem: *It is fall! I found 10 yellow leaves. I gave 7 to my friend. How many leaves are left?*

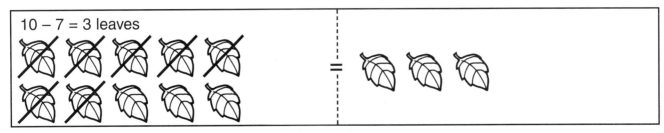

Math

Holiday Math Wizard Problems

Use these problems, featuring favorite holidays, to reinforce the seasons and months of the year.

January Holidays
January 1—New Year's Day

5 friends came to my New Year's party. 3 had to leave early. How many friends are left?

I made 2 snowmen. My friends made 6 more snowmen. How many snowmen in all?

February Holidays
February 2—Groundhog Day
February 14—Valentine's Day

I have 9 valentines. I will give 5 away. How many valentines are left?

It is winter. I saw 6 groundhogs looking for their shadows. 3 more groundhogs came. How many groundhogs in all?

March Holidays
March 17—St. Patrick's Day

Spring is here! There are 9 birds in a tree. 4 more come. How many birds in all?

7 leprechauns meet at the rainbow. 3 leprechauns leave. How many leprechauns are left?

April Holidays
Easter Sunday

I hid 8 Easter eggs. 7 eggs were found. How many eggs are left?

I saw 11 bunnies. 3 more bunnies came. How many bunnies in all?

May Holidays
Last Monday—Memorial Day

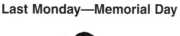

10 flowers are blooming in my garden. I picked 5 for my mom. How many flowers are left?

There are 3 bands at the beginning of the Memorial Day parade. There are 4 more bands at the end. How many bands in all?

June Holidays
June 14—Flag Day

There are 9 flags flying in the breeze. 3 flags are taken down. How many flags are left?

8 flags are posted in my neighborhood. 8 more flags are put up. How many flags in all?

Holiday Math Wizard Problems *(cont.)*

### July Holidays **July 4—Independence Day**	### August Holidays **None**	### September Holidays **First Monday—Labor Day**

It is summer. 15 frogs are swimming. 7 frogs jump out of the water. How many frogs are left?

It is the Fourth of July. We are popping firecrackers. We popped 4 firecrackers. Then we popped 6 more. How many firecrackers in all?

There are 5 birthday parties in August. I've already been to 3 of them. How many parties are left?

It's party time! I have 12 cupcakes. Mom makes 12 more. How many cupcakes in all?

There are 2 teachers working. 8 more teachers come to help. How many teachers in all?

It is fall! I found 17 red leaves. I gave 5 to my friend. How many leaves are left?

### October Holidays **October 12—Columbus Day** **October 31—Halloween**	### November Holidays **November 11—Veteran's Day** **Last Thursday Thanksgiving**	### December Holidays **December 25—Christmas Day** **Hanukkah**

3 ships came to America. 1 ship went back. How many ships are left?

9 pumpkins were sitting on my porch. Mom brought 1 more pumpkin home. How many pumpkins in all?

8 soldiers are marching. 3 more joined them. How many soldiers in all?

10 turkeys were cooked for Thanksgiving. 7 turkeys were eaten. How many turkeys are left?

I have 7 candy sticks. Santa brings me 5 more. How many candy sticks in all?

There are 16 gifts for Hanukkah. We gave 3 gifts to friends. How many gifts are left?

Calendar Capers

Use the calendar to solve the math problems below.

| | | | January | | | |
S	M	T	W	T	F	S
			1	2	3	4
5	6	7	8	9	10	11
12	13	14	15	16	17	18
19	20	21	22	23	24	25
26	27	28	29	30	31	

1. The month of the year on the calendar is _____.

2. There are _____ days in the month of January.

3. There are _____ Wednesdays in this month.

4. There are _____ Sundays in this month.

5. What day of the week is January 21? _____

6. The second Thursday is January _____.

7. The third Monday is January _____.

8. The last day of the month is on _____.

9. The first day of the month is on _____.

10. January has _____ full weeks.

Bonus: If there are 12 days left in the month of January, what is today's date?

When Seasons Begin

Summer Solstice

The first day of summer in the northern hemisphere is called the summer solstice and occurs around June 21. On this day, the North Pole is tilted closest to the sun. The summer solstice is the longest day of the year. In the northern hemisphere, the days before and after the summer solstice get direct sunlight for a longer amount of time, causing the warm temperatures of summer.

Winter Solstice

The first day of winter for the northern hemisphere is called the winter solstice and occurs around December 21. On this day, the North Pole is tilted farthest away from the sun. The winter solstice is the shortest day of the year. In the northern hemisphere, the days before and after the winter solstice get direct sunlight for a lesser amount of time, causing the cold temperatures of winter.

Vernal and Autumnal Equinox

Equinox literally means "equal night." On the day of the vernal (spring) equinox and the autumnal (fall) equinox, day and night are about the same length all over the world. During the vernal and autumnal equinoxes, the heat from the sun is about equal on both halves of Earth.

The beginning of spring in the northern hemisphere is marked by the vernal equinox that occurs around March 21. The beginning of fall in the northern hemisphere is marked by the autumnal equinox that occurs around September 23.

Opposite Seasons

Because Earth tilts on an axis, the northern and southern hemispheres have exactly opposite seasons. When the northern hemisphere has spring, the southern hemisphere has fall. When the northern hemisphere has summer, the southern hemisphere has winter.

Tropical Regions around the equator and Polar Regions around the North and South Poles have very little change in temperature and climate, and do not have the four climatic seasons of spring, summer, fall, and winter. These regions have two seasons. The Tropical Regions have a wet season and a dry season, and the Polar Regions have a light season and a dark season.

Life Cycle of a Robin

All About Robins: Spring is the time of the year when baby birds are born. The American Robin has dark brown feathers with a bright reddish brown breast. Each spring, these birds usually raise two or three broods (each brood has three or four babies). Robins feed mainly on fruit and like to build their nests in fruit trees just like the robins in *The Apple Pie Tree*.

Materials (for each student):

- copy of Life Cycle Pictures (page 72)
- crayons
- scissors
- glue

Directions:

Color the Life Cycle Pictures. Cut out the pictures and glue them in order (from 1–4) on the circle below.

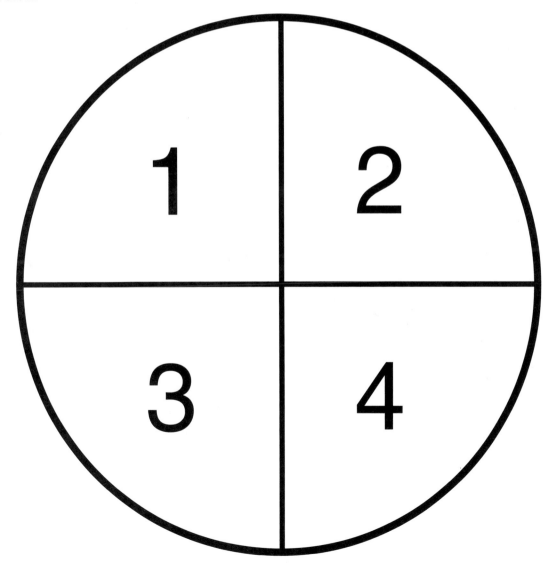

Life Cycle Pictures

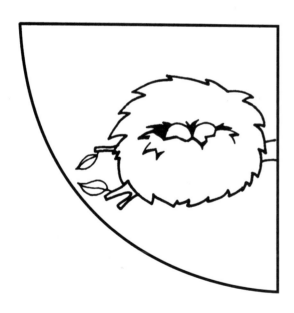

72

Solar System Calendar

Group Activity

Have the students imagine that they live on a new planet where the days, months, and seasons are different from Earth's. Brainstorm and write the answers to the questions below on a chart or board for students to use during the activity. Have students create a calendar page to go with the new planet.

(**Note:** Keep the days and months within a manageable range for developing the calendar. The days in a month should fit on one sheet of paper.)

The name of our planet is_____.

The months on our planet are_____ days long.

There are _____ (1 month for each child in the class) months in a year on our planet.

The seasons on our planet are_____ months long.

There are _____seasons on our planet.

There are _____days in a year on our planet.

The days on our planet are _____hours long.

Independent Activity

Have the students design a calendar month for the imaginary planet in a new shape, such as a square or triangle. Encourage them to invent new names for the days of the week and the month. Have them select one day on their calendar and create a special holiday for that day.

When finished, have each student show his or her calendar to the class and tell about the calendar and the special holiday created.

Extension

Extend the activity by asking the students to write and illustrate a short story about life on the imaginary planet.

Marshmallow Equinox

Read and discuss When Seasons Begin on page 70 before students make the Marshmallow Equinox.

Materials (amount for each student):

- 1 marshmallow, cut in half
- 1 paper muffin cup with orange drink powder
- 1 paper muffin cup with chocolate drink powder
- a wax paper work area

Directions:

Remind students that equinox means equal night and on the day of spring or fall equinox, the day and night are the same length. Tell students that they will construct a replica of Earth at equinox using a marshmallow and drink colors. (The orange color will represent day and the brown color will represent night.) On the wax paper, pour some orange powder and some brown powder so they aren't touching. Students roll one-half of the marshmallow in the orange powder and the other half in the chocolate. Then they will push the marshmallow back together to show the equal night and day of the equinox. After everyone is finished, clean up is easy. Eat the Marshmallow Equinox and throw everything else away. (Check for allergies before allowing children to eat.)

(**Note:** Dampening the marshmallow will help the powder stick and children love it when they get to lick it before adding the powder.)

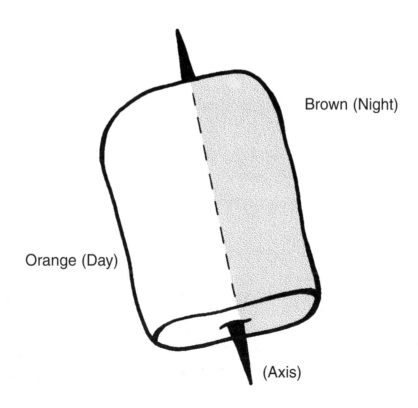

Brown (Night)

Orange (Day)

(Axis)

Feed the Hungry Birds

During winter, fruit, seeds, and insects that birds usually eat are hard to find. Students can help birds survive through the cold winter months by making bird feeders for winter birds.

Pinecone Bird Feeder

Materials:

- 1 large pinecone
- 6" (15 cm) piece of wire
- craft stick
- birdseed
- Something sticky, such as soy butter, peanut butter, or shortening

Directions:

Wrap the wire around the stem of the pinecone to make a hanger. Use the craft stick to cover the pinecone with soy butter. Roll the pinecone in the birdseed. Hang the pinecone outside in a protected area to keep rainwater from washing the soy butter and seeds away. (Be sure to hang the feeder where birds can easily find it.)

Milk Carton Bird Feeder

Materials:

- half-gallon milk carton
- birdseed
- strong yarn or twine
- paint and paintbrushes (optional)

Directions:

Before the activity, cut large squares in the four sides of the milk carton as shown. (Teachers need to cut these holes.) Punch a hole through the top and tie the yarn through the hole to form a hanger. The bird feeders can be left as they are, or the students can paint them. Fill the feeders with birdseed; then hang them outside to feed the winter birds.

Songs for Days, Months, and Seasons

These songs and movement activities will help students remember the months, seasons, and days of the week.

(Patty cake with a partner while chanting the song.)

Sunday—one, *(Clap your hands, patty cake both hands.)*

Monday—two, *(Clap your hands, patty cake right hands.)*

Tuesday—three, *(Clap your hands, patty cake left hands.)*

Wednesday—four, *(Clap your hands, patty cake both hands.)*

Thursday—five, *(Clap your hands, patty cake right hands.)*

Friday—six, *(Clap your hands, patty cake left hands.)*

Saturday—seven, *(Clap your hands, patty cake both hands.)*

Seven days of the week. *(Clap your hands seven times.)*

There are seven days,
There are seven days,
There are seven days in a week.
Sunday, Monday, Tuesday,
Wednesday,
Thursday, Friday, Saturday.
(Sing to the tune of "Oh My Darling, Clementine.")

Today is _____.
Today is _____.
All day long, all day long.
Yesterday was_____.
Tomorrow is _____.
Oh, what fun. Oh, what fun!
(Sing to the tune of "Frere Jacques.")

There are seven days in a week,
Seven days in a week,
Seven days in a week,
And I can name them all.
Sunday, Monday, Tuesday,
Wednesday, Thursday, Friday,
Saturday is the last day,
And I have named them all.
(Sing to the tune of "For He's a Jolly Good Fellow.")

Come along and sing with me,
There are seven days you see,
Sunday, Monday, Tuesday, too,
Wednesday, Thursday, just for you.
Friday, Saturday, that's the end,
Then the week starts over again.
(Sing to the tune of "Twinkle, Twinkle, Little Star.")

January *(Put right hand in front, palm down.)* February *(Put left hand in front, palm down.)*

March *(Put right hand in front, palm up.)* And April *(Put left hand in front, palm up.)*

May *(Move right hand to left shoulder.)* June *(Move left hand to right shoulder.)*

July *(Move right hand to head.)* August *(Move left hand to head.)*

September *(Move right hand to left hip.)* October *(Move left hand to right hip.)*

November *(Move right hand to right hip.)* December *(Move left hand to left hip.)*

Oh . . . the months of the year. *(Wiggle hips from side to side.)*

(Jump a ¼ turn to the right. Repeat actions and turns four times until you reach the original position.)

(Sing to the tune of "Macarena.")

Songs for Days, Months, and Seasons *(cont.)*

Is it spring? *(Place hands on head.)*
Is it summer? *(Place hands on shoulders.)*
Is it fall or is it winter? *(Place hands on knees.)*
There are four . . . seasons in a year,
(Hold up four fingers.)
Just what season is it here?
(Sing to the tune of "This Old Man.")

Come along and sing with me,
There are four seasons you see.
Spring and summer it is true,
Fall and winter just for you.
Four seasons that's the end,
Then they start all over again.
(Sing to the tune of "Twinkle, Twinkle, Little Star.")

There are four seasons,
There are four seasons,
There are four seasons in a year.
Spring, summer, fall, and winter,
There are four seasons in a year.
(Sing to the tune of "Oh My Darling, Clementine.")

January, February,
March and April,
May, June,
July and August,
September, October,
November and December,
Twelve months in a year.
(Sing to the tune of "Ten Little Indians.")

There are twelve months in a year,
Twelve months in a year,
Twelve months in a year,
And I can name them all.
January, February, March,
April, May, and June,
That's six of the months,
And I can name them all.
July, August, September,
October, November, December,
That's all twelve months,
And I have named them all.
(Sing to the tune of "For He's a Jolly Good Fellow.")

There are four seasons in a year,
Four seasons in a year,
Four seasons in a year,
And I can name them all.
Spring is the first season,
Then summer and fall,
Winter is the last season,
And I have named them all.
(Sing to the tune of "For He's a Jolly Good Fellow.")

Bibliography

Books by Maurice Sendak

Chicken Soup with Rice. HarperCollins Children's Books, 1990.

In the Night Kitchen. HarperCollins Publishers, 1995.

Nutshell Library. HarperCollins Children's Books, 1976.

Where the Wild Things Are. HarperCollins Children's Books, 1984.

Books by Zoe Hall

The Apple Pie Tree. Scholastic Inc., 1996.

Fall Leaves Fall! Scholastic Inc., 1999.

It's Pumpkin Time! Scholastic Inc., 1999.

Surprise Garden. Scholastic Inc., 1998.

Days, Months, and Seasons

Aruego, Jose *Alligators and Others All Year Long.* Macmillian Books, 1993.

Barrett, Judith. *Cloudy With a Chance of Meatballs.* Simon and Shuster, 1982.

Bernard, Robin. *Trees for all Seasons.* National Geographic Society, 2001.

Borden, Louise. *Caps, Hats, Socks,and Mittens*: *A Book About the Four Seasons*
Scholastic Inc., 1991.

Branley, Franklyn M. *Sunshine Makes the Seasons.* HarperCollins Children's Books,1989.

Bruchac, Joseph and London, Jonathon. *Thirteen Moons on Turtle's Back: A Native American
Year of Moons.* Putman Juvenile.

Carle, Eric. *Dream Show.* Philomel Books, 2000.

Carle, Eric. *Today Is Monday.* Penguin Putman Books for Young Readers, 2001.

Cousins, Lucy. *Maisy's Seasons.* Candlewick Press, 2002.

Gibbons, Gail. *The Reason for the Seasons.* Holiday House, Inc., 1996.

Gibbons, Gail. *The Seasons of Arnold's Apple Tree.* Harcourt, 1991.

Katz, Karen. *Twelve Hats for Lena.* Simon & Schuster Children's Books, 2002.

Keats, Ezra Jack. *Snowy Day.* Viking Press, 1996.

Milnes, Ellen. *Mickey's Day of the Week.* Random House Disney, 1999.

Monroe, Mary A. *The Four Seasons.* Harlequin Enterprises, 2001.

Web Connections

To access lesson plans and activities for the months and seasons, go to any search engine and type "months" or "seasons." One of the best sites for lesson plans and information on any subject is **http://www.askeric.org** .

Appendix

Pages 6–7
Rhyming Words Chart

January	n<u>ice</u>	<u>ice</u>	r<u>ice</u>	tw<u>ice</u>
February	b<u>e</u>	anniversar<u>y</u>	m<u>e</u>	
March	d<u>oor</u>	fl<u>oor</u>	m<u>ore</u>	
April	aw<u>ay</u>	Bomb<u>ay</u>	d<u>ay</u>	
May	b<u>est</u>	n<u>est</u>		
June	gr<u>oup</u>	dr<u>oop</u>	s<u>oup</u>	
July	p<u>eep</u>	d<u>eep</u>	ch<u>eap</u>	
August	h<u>ot</u>	p<u>ot</u>	n<u>ot</u>	
September	wh<u>ile</u>	crocod<u>ile</u>	N<u>ile</u>	
October	h<u>ost</u>	gh<u>ost</u>	t<u>oast</u>	
November	g<u>ale</u>	t<u>ail</u>	wh<u>ale</u>	
December	b<u>e</u>	tr<u>ee</u>	m<u>e</u>	

*(The words **twice** and **rice** are repeated on almost every page.)*

Pages 6–7
Ordinal Number Chart

Month	Ordinal Number	Season	Picture
January	first/1st	winter	ice skates
February	second/2nd	winter	snowman
March	third/3rd	spring	wind
April	fourth/4th	spring	rain
May	fifth/5th	spring	bird
June	sixth/6th	summer	flower
July	seventh/7th	summer	fireworks
August	eighth/8th	summer	sun
September	ninth/9th	fall	falling leaves
October	tenth/10th	fall	pumpkin
November	eleventh/11th	fall	turkey
December	twelfth/12th	winter	gifts

Page 7
Vocabulary Development—Special Words

sipping, anniversary, twice, laps, roars, Spain, Bombay, concocting, group, droop, sprinkle, once, crocodile, Nile, whoopy, gale, spouting, baubled, bangled

Page 28
Season Chart

Spring	Summer	Fall	Winter
March, April, May	**June, July, August**	**September, October, November**	**December, January, February**
baseball	swimming	colored leaves	snow
cool	hot	cool	cold

Answer Key

Page 62

Page 63

Days of the Week—Friday, Saturday, Thursday, Tuesday, Monday, Wednesday, Sunday

Seasons of the Year—fall, winter, summer, spring

Months of the Year—July, March, May, November, October, April, August, December, September, January, June, February

Page 64

Across—
2. March
5. April
10. September

4. June
6. November
11. August

Down—
1. January
4. July
8. May

3. December
7. October
9. February

Page 65

1. 7 days
2. 4 seasons
3. 12 months
4. Sunday, Monday, Tuesday, Wednesday, Thursday, Friday, Saturday
5. spring, summer, fall, winter
6. December, January, February
7. April, May
8. September, October, November
9. June, July

Pages 67–68

January—2 friends/8 snowmen

February—4 valentines/9 groundhogs

March—13 birds/4 leprechauns

April—1 egg/14 bunnies

May—5 flowers/7 bands

June—6 flags/16 flags

July—8 frogs/10 firecrackers

August—2 parties/24 cupcakes

September—10 teachers/12 leaves

October—2 ships/10 pumpkins

November—11 soldiers/3 turkeys

December—12 candy sticks/13 gifts

Page 69

1. January
2. 31 days
3. 5 Wednesdays
4. 4 Sundays
5. Tuesday
6. January 9th
7. January 20th
8. Friday
9. Wednesday
10. 3 full weeks
Bonus: January 19th

#3106 Thematic Unit—Months and Seasons   80   *©Teacher Created Materials, Inc.*